WISLEY HANDB

GW00937920

# Roses

S. M. GAULT

LONDON
The Royal Horticultural Society
Reprinted 1981

# Contents

*Photographs by Ernest Crowson, R. P. Scase, R. J. Corbin and Harry Smith Collection.*

# Roses

Much of the pleasure which gardening gives can be obtained from growing roses. Few other groups of plants have such a long flowering period or such diversity of character or can be used in so many ways. Roses vary from plants a few inches high to scramblers which with suitable support, such as an old tree, will attain 40 feet (12m) in height.

This diversity in habit is excelled by the flowers, from singles, exquisite in their four or five petalled simplicity, through many forms, especially in the "old garden roses", to the symmetrically spiralled hybrid tea, so beloved by exhibitors. Nor does it end there, for have we not fruits also, the hips of late summer and autumn? Lovelier than any, unsurpassed by those of any tree or shrub are the large orange scarlet fruits of *R. moyesii* and its relations. Many others are highly decorative in the garden or flower arrangements, from the small oval hips of *R. helenae* to the somewhat more vulgar but very showy tomato-like hips of *R. rugosa*. Many of the floribundas, especially those with a limited number of petals, will also provide a display in the autumn if dead-heading is not too rigidly practised. This small book is designed to serve as an introduction to roses, to whet the appetite of the beginner in the hope that given time you will explore further and find interest in "old ones and new ones, loved ones and neglected ones". I have had great pleasure in growing roses over many years. I hope the reader may partake of it, too.

## 1. Soils for roses

The fallacy that roses grow best on clay soils, indeed will only do well on them, still persists in some quarters. Roses will grow on most soils, but they are not bog plants and will only thrive on soils which are adequately drained. Likewise the most popular groups, those of the hybrid teas and floribundas are not generally happy on bare, hungry chalk, although even this type of soil can be improved sufficiently to grow some roses.

Taking over a new garden can be an exciting exercise. But the type of soil will be a major factor in what can be grown. A heavy sticky clay soil should if possible be avoided. In such a soil water does not readily drain away, and therefore it is sticky and wet, hard to cultivate and heavy to dig. In very dry weather the soil shrinks, resulting in large cracks, further drying and consequent root damage. Potentially, clay soils are rich in plant foods and these are made more easily available by adding humus to the soil such as partially decayed leaves or compost, or strawy manure: this opens up the soil structure, allowing better root penetration. To improve clay is hard work, for all these materials must be thoroughly mixed in during digging with spade or fork. But the advantages are that when root growth is good plants get adequate food and water.

Lime has the ability to break down clay but it may also increase the alkaline reaction of the soil too much: roses like a slightly acid soil. As an alternative to liming, dressings of coarse sand, road grit, bonfire ash, peat and gypsum all improve clay soils without increasing alkalinity. Gypsum is particularly useful if well forked in at 8 oz. per square yard, a method I found most suitable with London clay in Queen Mary's Garden, Regents Park. The use of peat has become universal, being easily obtainable at some cost. Use a coarse grade, leaving some on the surface where it renders planting and movement more comfortable.

Light or sandy soils are totally different to clay being composed of coarse particles. They drain quickly, so can be cultivated soon after heavy rain, but this rapid drainage is often wasteful especially in summer. In order to improve such soils large quantities of farmyard manure or good compost are required to help to retain water and plant nutrients. As plant foods are soluble this is important, otherwise much will be lost through too rapid drainage. Unfortunately nowadays good well rotted farmyard manure is likely to be scarce even in country districts and unobtainable in towns. Compost is rarely available in sufficient quantity so peat is the most useful alternative. But it needs the addition of a balanced fertilizer for a good result to be obtained. The soil most desired by gardeners is good loam, in which the clay and sand particles are balanced and there is sufficient humus to ensure greater fertility plus the ability to retain plant foods, rather than allow them to drain away. The value of humus in the soil has long been recognised for many garden plants and it certainly applies for roses. There is little that needs to be done to a loam to prepare it for rose planting.

# 2. Preparation for planting

In a small garden pre-planting cultivation with hand tools is probably still the best, although in these days when rotovators or other machines can be hired the hard physical work can be lightened and the time needed for proper cultivation can be reduced. The old method of trenching and breaking up the soil to a depth of three feet undoubtedly produced good results but is not really necessary. Digging to one spade's depth and breaking up of the spit underneath, will provide twenty inches of soil (50cm) in which the roses can extend their roots and this should be ample.

If the site is a new one, skim off the turf (a layer of about 2 inches) chop it up and work it into the soil to a depth of at least 10 inches (25cm) where it will gradually rot and be a valuable source of humus. This can be augmented by digging in well-rotted farmyard manure, still the ideal material when obtainable, but usually difficult in towns. Well-rotted garden compost is also excellent but not readily available, being generally prepared in established gardens where the necessary materials can be gathered. Dried compost or sludges are available from some municipal authorities; these are generally low in potash content, but this can be added as sulphate of potash. In some cases chemicals harmful to plants may be present in materials produced by industrial processes and an analysis should be obtained and enquiries made regarding source of the material before buying them.

In these days most people with an interest in plants know something of the value of peat, so much has been written about it. It does not appear to be so well understood that peat although improving the texture of soil and adding humus does not provide any plant food. This can be overcome by adding an organic fertilizer, such as hoof and horn meal, which if used at 2 to 3 ounces per square yard (66-100g/m²) will slowly release plant food throughout the growing season.

On light soils or those which are well drained the incorporation of humus-forming materials will lift the level of the beds so some of the poorer sub-soil should be removed to make allowance for this. I have already mentioned the difficulty of growing some types of roses where chalk is the main ingredient. Breaking up the chalk and removing it is a laborious job unless the garden is of sufficient size to allow machine operations. The alternative is to build up on top with good soil, although this can bring difficulties too in dry seasons. Possibly the best solution is to remove some chalk, breaking up the remainder, and incorporate some

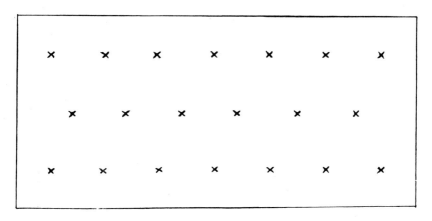

Fig. 1.    A bed for twenty roses, spaced at twelve inches from the sides of the bed and at eighteen inches between the plants (30 × 45cm).

5

good top soil, with added organic matter. This is a daunting prospect only to be undertaken by an enthusiast.

Another daunting prospect may face a new owner who has taken over a garden in which roses have been grown for many years. Here the problem is a rose-sick soil, a well known condition, for which the only solution seems to be to plant the roses in fresh soil. Commercial rose growers overcome this problem by rotating their crop and sometimes fallowing for a season, measures which are difficult to carry out in the average small garden. In gardens where space is available cutting out and preparing new beds is the most obvious solution, or if you have a vegetable garden changing over the soil is another possibility. Buying in fresh top soil may also be considered. It is necessary to change the top spit of old soil completely; to do less is a waste of time and effort.

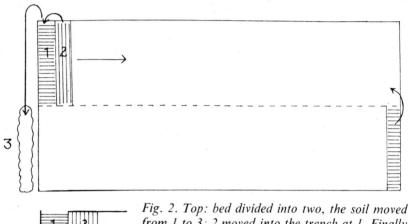

Fig. 2. Top: bed divided into two, the soil moved from 1 to 3: 2 moved into the trench at 1. Finally the soil at 3 used to fill the last trench
Left: Side view of the bed: trench 2 is moved into trench 1 after the second layer has been broken up with a fork

Dazomet, a soil sterilant, has been used with considerable success in gardens too large in scale to consider changing over the soil: formaldehyde is also recommended. The soil is cleared and cultivated in the autumn; the sterilant can then be applied and is rendered more effective if covered with polythene for some weeks. Planting can then be carried out in spring.

It is a useful long term idea with rectangular beds to allow a plot of grass similar in size to remain between the beds. A bed of roses should, if well looked after, last for fifteen years. Then to overcome the soil sickness problem you can use the space between for fresh beds and grass over the old ones.

On taking over a garden, some planning is necessary or at least a rough plan to help to formulate your ideas. Most gardens are viewed from the house, and therefore, should be planned from there. The popular types of roses are generally most effective when planted in beds of reasonable size, so it is better to have one good sized bed than several small ones, which are more difficult to maintain. Simple beds are easier to design and plant, so confine yourself to rectangles or square or even circular beds. Rectangular beds are in general easier to start with and can be marked out with some pegs in the corners joined up by string to outline the size of the bed. The size of the bed should be determined by the number of roses it is intended to grow, bearing in mind that planting can be done more effectively with a staggered planting of roses (see Fig. 1).

By splitting the bed in two some soil shifting can be avoided. This is the time too, to incorporate humus in the soil as already mentioned, working some into the lower spit as well. It will be found on completion that the bed will be higher than before digging but the soil will gradually settle and should be allowed to do so before planting. Some rain will help to consolidate the bed but if there seems to be a danger of the bed becoming too wet cover it with a sheet of polythene. Generally speaking an interval of a month between preparation and planting should be allowed for settlement of the soil.

# 3. Choosing plants

When selecting a rose in the garden shop or centre look for one with at least two good branches which should be firm and well ripened (this can be ascertained by pressing between thumb and finger, in the right condition there will be no yielding). Some varieties may produce more growths, an added bonus where the root system is adequate. Selection of varieties is dependent on your requirements and visits to local gardens or a rose specialist's nursery, if you are fortunate to have one near, will give an indication of how certain varieties behave in your area.

Roses are now sold in containers by specialist growers and also by garden centres, giving an opportunity especially to the newcomer to select roses which appeal to them. In addition to selecting a variety which appeals to your taste, select good healthy looking plants well established in the container, probably just showing roots coming out through the bottom.

Many experienced rosarians have their own favourite suppliers who can be relied on to produce well-grown plants, that have been allowed ample room in the nursery. Even so mistakes can occur and the nurseryman should be informed so that any such mistake can be rectified, a service unlikely to be performed when a plant is purchased from stores.

Many roses are bought from stores; these will give good results but sometimes these packaged plants may be induced into premature growth by a higher temperature which results in blanched shoots. These are no bargain however cheap the plants may be and are best avoided.

Many growers have good catalogues, with entrancing pictures of perfect roses. If such varieties appear in several catalogues it is safe to assume that the variety is in demand and likely to be satisfactory. But if possible see roses growing as well; visits during the rose season to such gardens as Queen Mary's rose garden in Regent's Park in London, to the Royal National Rose Society's garden at St Albans in Hertfordshire and the RHS Garden near Woking in Surrey will show a wide range of all kinds of roses growing. There are many parks in towns all over the country where a selection of modern varieties can also be seen.

# 4. Planting

Before starting to plant, it is quite a useful idea to mark with a short cane where each tree is to be planted so as to ensure even distribution over the bed and I always prefer staggered planting. Distance of planting will depend on the cultivar; many modern roses are satisfactorily spaced at 18 inches apart between the bushes and the rows (45cm). For more vigorous cultivars this distance can be extended by 3 to 6 inches (15cm). If the bushes are to be underplanted with other plants, (see p.25) a system which extends the season of interest and, dare I say it, the beauty of the garden, the wider spacing should be used. Allow a distance of 12 inches (30cm) between the outside row of plants and the edge of the bed.

Many roses are now available at garden shops and garden centres in containers so that planting may be done at any time of year, even in flower. Such roses should have been grown in a container or well established in it so that the root ball is firm, and not liable to fall apart when the plant is removed. Containerised roses which have been just lifted from the open ground and placed in the container ready for sale are not properly established and should not be bought. Plant into well prepared ground (see above), into a hole large enough to take the whole root ball and the container placed in it at the correct depth. When in position slip a sharp knife round the base of the container (plastic) and remove the base by sliding it out from underneath. Then slit up the plastic container at the side and remove. Treated thus the root ball will be kept intact so that soil can be filled in and firmed in the usual way. It is a mistake to try and spread roots as this is liable to cause disturbance. Care must always be taken to see that the root ball is reasonably moist before planting; if not ensure this by a thorough watering.

Generally, container grown plants are grown in nurseries or garden centres when planting in the growing season with some form of irrigation, so it is important to continue watering until the rose is established. This is particularly important in spring or early summer when wind or hot sun

*Fig. 3. A rose bush as sent from the nursery.*

*Fig. 4. The same bush with roots and stems pruned before planting.*

*Fig. 5. The same rose bush in the planting hole showing how the roots are spread out. The cane across the hole shows where the soil level should be when planting is finished.*

9

may affect the plants and cause them to wilt. In warm weather a good spray over the plants in the evenings will contribute much to the welfare of the plants and their establishment. Check up to ensure soil remains firm round the root ball, especially on heavy soils in dry weather.

The same principles apply when planting from a container in the winter, although then watering in is not usually necessary. I still think that planting dormant trees from the end of October onwards is likely to produce the best results and this is the time of year when the "bare root" bushes are sent out from mail-order nurserymen. Transplanting at this time, when there is no top growth, is less of a shock to the plant.

The earlier the planting is done the better, but often the nurserymen are not able to lift the roses for despatching to customers until November or December. Planting can be continued up to and including March, so long as soil conditions are good, that is, not too wet or frozen. If the plants arrive when the soil conditions are bad, unpack them and make sure they have not become dry on their journey. If they are dry place the plants in a tank, bath or container of water for several hours, overnight will not harm them. They can then be "heeled in". This is best done by digging out a trench 12 inches deep (30cm) in which the bushes are laid, the roots well covered with soil which is then firmed making sure that the area where roots and top growth meet (see Fig. 5) is well covered. The roses can remain in this situation for several weeks until planting conditions become favourable.

Planting should be carefully carried out, taking care to ensure that the union between the rootstock and the stem of the tree is covered by an inch or so of soil. This union can be easily recognized by a bulge or knot where the "bud" has been inserted in the rootstock. A hole large enough to accommodate the roots comfortably should be taken out and after cutting back any damaged roots place the plant slightly deeper in the hole. It is a good plan to have some damp peat available in which hoof and horn meal or bone-meal has been mixed, and this can be shaken in around the roots before returning some of the soil. Shake the plant gently to ensure that the soil has settled round the roots, before being trodden in. Do not fill in the soil fully until this has been done, when it can be completed by treading and then the whole bed lightly forked over.

Many rosarians like to grow a few standards, to add some height to their beds, so some beginners may like to follow suit. Full standards have 42 inch (1.05m) stems, and half standards 30 inch (75cm) stems. If suitable to your taste, therefore, standards should be planted before the bush trees. Before planting the standards, however, it is best to insert good sound stakes driven at least 12 inches (30cm) into the ground with 2½ or or 3½ feet (75-105cm) above ground to ensure stability. Many standards are grown on *Rosa rugosa* stems, and these can generally be identified by numerous small prickles. It is important that deep planting is not carried out or there will be trouble with suckers.

Examination of a standard grown on a *rugosa* stem will show two or three flat layers of fibrous roots. In order that the bottom layers are not planted too deeply it is usually necessary to carry out the somewhat drastic treatment of removing the upper layer close to the stem. It is sufficient to cover the roots with 2 or 3 inches (5-7cm) of soil; a cane placed across the hole at the natural level of the soil will give you a guide. You can then ensure that planting will be at the correct level by tying the standard to the stake, before filling in the soil.

**Fertilizers**
The main foods required for plants are nitrogen, phosphorus and potassium. The use of a special rose fertilizer is in general most convenient for the beginner. Such fertilizers contain all three nutrients, and the proportions are indicated on the bag. Some minor elements are also required. These are included in compound fertilizers and are also to be found in organic manures especially in good farmyard manure. The valuable portion of nutrient purchased as a compound fertilizer and shown in the analysis is that shown as soluble. The insoluble part is not available immediately indeed may never become available.

Nitrogen is essential for rose growth, but high doses should be avoided, as these induce soft growth which is susceptible to disease infection. Late summer application of nitrogen must be avoided because the end of the summer is the time for ripening the year's shoots, and any extra boost to growth will produce more soft shoots likely to die back in winter. Nitrogen is generally supplied as sulphate of ammonia, which will increase soil acidity, and therefore some growers prefer to use Nitro-chalk which is easy to apply, without increasing soil acidity, and produces quick results. Bonemeal has long been in favour with rose growers and is especially useful if mixed with damp peat to put around the roots of roses when planting. It is best applied in autumn to established plants, as it breaks down slowly to produce its nutrients. Bonemeal provides a little nitrogen with a slowly available supply of phosphate, which stimulates root growth. The general health of the plant is promoted by phosphates especially in districts of high rainfall as an aid to ripened growth. In compound fertilizers superphosphate is generally used as the source of phosphorus. Potash is important in many plants but particularly in roses, it counteracts soft growth and aids ripening, essential in the production of hard ripe wood likely to come safely through severe winter weather. It also improves the substance and colour of the flowers. There is usually some potash present to some degree in heavy soils but it is required on light soils, especially so on chalky soils. It is possible to give a combination spray to roses every 10 to 14 days: one tested combination is triforine (for mildew and black spot control) and dimethoate (for aphids), plus a foliar feed.

Quicker acting fertilizers may be most readily applied after pruning in February or March, forking them into the soil to avoid leaving them on

11

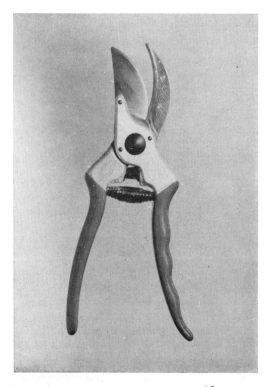

*Fig. 6. Four pruning cuts on rose stems; the right hand stem is pruned correctly. The other cuts are (left) too ragged, (centre) too high leaving a snag, (right) too low leaving the bud projecting.*

*Fig. 7. A pair of garden secateurs, one of several types available.*

12

the surface. Generally it is unwise to stimulate further growth in roses by applying fertilizers after the end of July, the exception being very wet seasons. These can induce soft growth which can be counteracted by a potash dressing. Most fertilizers can be applied safely at the rate of 1 oz per sq. yd. (30 to 40g per m²). Directions are generally provided which may in some cases be twice this rate of application and can be followed safely but should not be exceeded.

# 5. Pruning

The beginner to rose growing may wonder why such an operation as pruning is necessary. Many roses today are grown in small gardens, often in beds cut in a lawn, so that unless some pruning is carried out, the roses will not only outgrow their position but become gaunt bushes and lose their ornamental value. In unpruned bushes, the quality of bloom deteriorates, and the bush becomes top heavy, liable to be blown about in stormy weather, especially in summer when heavy in leaf and flower, and, indeed, may then suffer irreparable damage to the root system.

It is clear, therefore, that some pruning is necessary in order to have healthy roses, and roses only look well if they are healthy. Remove all unproductive growth; dead and diseased wood comes into this category. It is also necessary for air and light to have access to the centre of the plant, so that diseases are not encouraged, and the shoots can be hardened before winter. This means the removal of crossing or impeding growths which clutter up the centre of the bush. Cutting back to an outward pointing bud will also keep the centre of the bush open, so take time to ensure the bud is pointing in the right direction before making a cut. Weak or damaged growths are unlikely to produce good blooms, and should also be removed. Good pruning requires no more time than bad pruning. Good pruning ensures that only good clean cuts are made (these heal more rapidly than ragged cuts) on the opposite side to the bud. A slightly sloping cut as seen in Figure 6 (right) will ensure water does not collect on the cut end and rot it. The cut should always clear the bud, so as not to damage it.

**Tools.** Some experienced rosarians prefer to prune with a good sharp knife and in skilled hands its superiority can scarcely be questioned. Few beginners will have either the skill to use a knife, however, or what is just as important, to keep it to the degree of sharpness required. For most rose growers, therefore, a pair of good secateurs, properly adjusted and kept clean and sharp is the most useful tool (Fig. 7). Many roses are well armed so that a pair of stout but flexible gloves is essential and a kneeling pad is useful for the over-fifties when removing old basal growths. Where growths have attained some size a pair of long-handled pruners or loppers will be found more useful. They will certainly be found more powerful when dealing with shrub roses. A narrow-bladed saw is even more useful when thick dead stems have to be removed from the base of the bush.

13

**When to prune.** The newcomer to rose growing may be somewhat mystified by varying opinions on the best time to prune. Gardeners generally are willing to advise and it should be possible in most cases to take advantage of local knowledge, preferably from successful growers. Personally I have never been an advocate of pruning by calendar, it is much better to be guided by and take advantage of the season and weather. Pruning is best done when weather is good, better for the plants and more comfortable for the operator. I always prefer to prune early, rather than late, so long as the roses are dormant or nearly so, but in general I like to have finished when March ends, so that the plant's energy is not wasted by bleeding or by cutting away newly produced young growths. While in charge of a large collection of roses I found it most practical to start pruning early in February, beginning with shrub roses, following with floribundas and ending up with the hybrid teas.

Pruning of large flowered and cluster-flowered bush roses early, will, in mild winters followed by an early spring tend to advance the time of flowering. The British climate is quite unpredictable at times so that a frost late in May can completely upset any programme. Gardens in town usually produce earlier flowers, temperatures being higher from the influence of central heated buildings than in the neighbouring countryside.

*Newly planted roses* should always be pruned fairly severely their first spring, especially bush types. Cut back each shoot to two or three buds from the base, removing very weak growths altogether if there are three good shoots on the bush. These should be sufficient to provide the new growths required, right from the bottom of the plant, thus ensuring a good start in building up a bush which will produce new basal replacement growths for each year. This is one of the secrets of success in producing a good and regular annual display. I have generally found autumn planting to be most successful but recognize that many amateurs with limited time find the lengthening days of March more convenient. At this time it is often easier to prune before planting, holding the bush in the hand.

Nowadays container-grown roses are very popular and they can be planted at any time. If planted in autumn or winter, at any time from October to April, they should be hard pruned. If bought after that the bushes should have been pruned at the nursery before sale. Even so it sometimes happens that the top bud does not grow as expected and growths are produced lower down. This occurs in established trees, too, on occasion; in such cases some further pruning is necessary, cutting back the stems close to the growths which have started. This eliminates unsightly snags, which not only spoil the appearance of the bushes, but are likely to result in further die-back.

*Established roses.* The large flowered (hybrid tea) group of roses is probably still the most popular for smaller gardens and established bushes are pruned according to the purpose for which the roses are grown. Thus exhibitors generally prune hard as advocated for newly planted roses,

14

*Fig. 8. A hybrid tea rose, before pruning.*

*Fig. 9. The same rose, after removal of old and centre wood.*

15

as this reduces the number of growths and consequently the number of flowers. The efforts of the plant are thus concentrated on a few, possibly larger flowers of good individual shape. In exposed gardens, particularly in the north, hard pruning becomes a compulsory exercise, especially after a severe winter, when the young growths may have become so severely frozen that sound wood can only be found near the base. When a shoot has been cut look at the colour of the pith, if white it is sound, if brown it is not and must be cut back further until live wood is reached.

As most gardeners are interested in garden display rather than exhibition blooms, lighter pruning has become more popular, because more flowers are produced, especially from such cultivars as 'Peace'. These robust growers tend to produce "blind" or flowerless shoots when severely pruned. Light pruning is carried out by removal of a third of the previous year's growth, as well as the removal of older wood where it has become congested. This system works very well with bushes on light soils, but on a heavy rich soil it soon produces very leggy, inelegant bushes which are liable to be blown about in stormy weather, so causing root damage. Eventually the stage is reached, sometimes after a particularly severe winter, when it becomes necessary to cut the bushes back to a foot or so above ground level. This is truly a frightening prospect for a beginner and is drastic treatment, but I have always found it works if all growths are cut back. The next year's crop will suffer of course and flower later but the plants should return to normal the following year.

In general I advocate the middle way of moderate pruning, pruning back to five or six eyes from the base of the previous year's growth and either removing or cutting hard back very weak and thin growths .Some cultivars produce shoots naturally from the base and if these growths are well ripened by autumn this provides an opportunity to replace an older growth, which should be removed completely. Where these natural breaks do not occur after some years the drastic treatment advocated above will then become necessary.

Floribunda roses (now called cluster-flowered roses) have become considerably more popular in recent years, particularly in public gardens and parks where masses of bloom and colour are required during summer and autumn. Many amateurs also appreciate these virtues and some are also interested in exhibiting them. In general this type of rose produces shoots more freely from the base, a trend which can be encouraged by the removal of older growths as opportunity arises. Young growths can be shortened by a third, older growths to five or six buds, or less in the compact growing cultivars which are now being produced. It is interesting to study different cultivars; by so doing differences in habit of growth become apparent and pruning for the best effect adjusted accordingly; thus a cultivar which tends to sprawl on the soil, may be better pruned to an inside eye to induce more upright growth. Many small thin growths also congest the bushes and are usually best removed altogether (see pp.18-19).

Standards, tall, or short, are much used by amateurs to lend height in a small garden. Prune according to the variety used, with a tendency to be rather on the severe side. I advocate this as very large heads are apt to suffer wind damage, and I always prune back to four or five buds. Weeping standards seem to have lost popularity but can be a nice central feature on a lawn. Generally the best "weepers" are the *wichuraiana* type ramblers which have only one flowering season; perhaps this is the reason for reduced interest. Pruning of this type of standard is very simple, just remove old flowering growths at the base when flowering has been completed, and there are sufficient young growths for replacement. Where there are not, shorten back the old flowering laterals to two eyes. Sometimes other types of roses are used for standards, in which case to be effective the main growths have to be tied down, and then shortening the flowering laterals to two or three buds will be enough.

Miniature roses are a special group which can be used in small gardens for beds or edging and are also useful for window boxes. Normally these cultivars are about 12 inches (30cm) in height and seem to me to be a little out of keeping with other roses, although with their own special appeal when used by themselves. Pruning presents no problem, the best results being produced if all weak growths are cut back hard or removed. Normal

*Fig. 11. The floribunda rose 'Iceberg', before pruning.*

*Fig. 12. After removal of old and central growth.*

*Fig. 13. Above. Pruning complete: hard pruning.*

*Fig. 14. Below. Pruning complete: moderate pruning.*

19

growths should be pruned back to four or five buds. Some cultivars occasionally produce one or two shoots so strong as to upset the symmetry of the plant, and removal of these will help to retain the compact habit expected in this type of rose.

Shrub roses may not be planted in such large numbers as large flowered or cluster-flowered types but have an invaluable part to play in many gardens, especially where there is room for larger plants. Many also provide beauty and fragrance over a long season, extending even into winter in some cases with displays of beautiful hips. Where these hips are valued it is obvious that no pruning should be done until the hips disappear. Pruning of shrub roses does not in general present much difficulty. They are treated as individual plants in which size and shape are important. In most cases flowers are most freely produced on growths formed the previous year so that any tendency to produce strong stems from near the base should be encouraged. Thus shoots which have flowered poorly may be removed even in summer after flowering to provide room for strong basal growths, and this may be supplemented by further thinning about February, or any time convenient when it is not cold and frosty.

Some of the modern shrub roses produce vigorous growths of considerable length which outgrow their fellows and in exposed borders the plants are apt to suffer from wind-rock. Shortening of such growths by a third will obviate this. Some old garden roses may suffer from mildew, particularly on the tips of young growths, and these are best removed below the infection and burned during the growing season.

Several repeat-flowering climbers have been produced by rose breeders in recent years, many of them very useful for covering up fences between gardens or for covering poles or tripods. These flower mainly on lateral growths which have been pruned to two or three buds after the flowering season is over. Some cultivars break freely from the base, always a desirable feature, and room for the new shoots may be provided by removal of an old growth. On poles or tripods, spiral training of the growths in near horizontal manner tends to help the production of basal growths and to induce a greater flower display. So freely do some of these cultivars produce their flowers, especially in autumn, that there is now a tendency to treat them as shrubs, by shortening the main growths.

Rambler roses, such as the well known 'Dorothy Perkins', with *Rosa wichuraiana* in its parentage, have lost favour because of their limited flowering season and other drawbacks. If the plants are in good health, enough young basal growths are generally produced to replace the old flowering growths, which can be removed as soon as flowering is over. The well known and still loved cultivars, 'Albertine' and 'Alberic Barbier', do not, however, produce basal growths to anything like the same extent so that many of the older growths must be retained and lateral shoots pruned back to a couple of buds. The occasional removal of

*Fig. 15. Right. A climbing rose before pruning.*

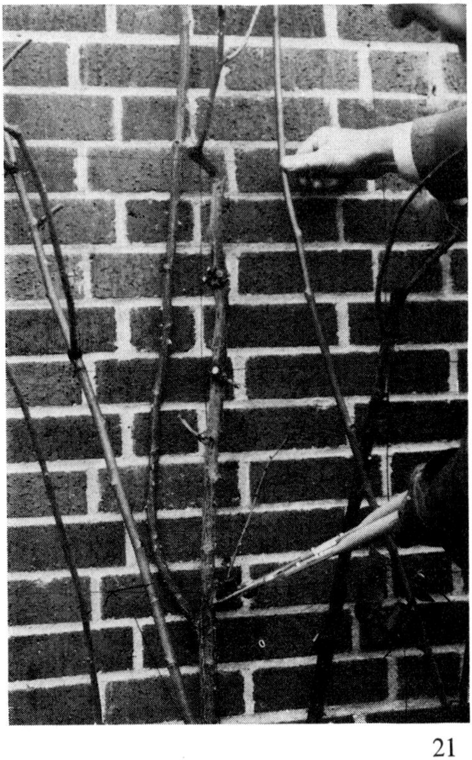

*Fig. 16. Left. Close-up of the same rose, showing the old worn-out stem with strong, new growth.*

*Fig. 17. Left. Climbing rose. Removing the old worn-out stem with loppers.*

*Fig. 18. Right. Pruning of the climbing rose completed, before tying-in.*

22

an old shoot will encourage the production of young growths, a renewal process which is always desirable with roses.

An alternative to pruning of some vigorous cultivars which produce strong shoots of 5 feet (1.5m) or so is training by pegging down, either to pegs driven firmly into the soil or to a framework parallel to the soil. An excellent example of this method can be seen at Wisley where the cultivars 'Uncle Walter' and 'Chinatown' are treated in this manner in the rose borders. When the flowering season is over, the pegged-down growths are cut away and replaced by those of the current year to provide the following season's display. This method induces most of the buds along the young growths to produce flowers, ensuring a wonderful display. Similarly roses of *wichuraiana* type can be used for banks or under trees quite horizontally.

Finally all prunings should be disposed of as soon as possible, preferably by burning. Other arrangements may have to be made in small town gardens, where bonfires are not allowed.

# 6. Summer treatment

Summer is the time when with the hard work of preparation, planting and pruning having been satisfactorily carried out, the gardener can begin to enjoy the display provided by the roses. When careful preparation has been carried out as advocated earlier, further feeding should not be required in the first year. In subsequent years, however, replacement of used plant food will be required. The beginner will find a proprietary brand of fertilizer specially compounded for roses is the most convenient method, and this should be applied as directed (see p.11). Two applications are worthwhile, the first after pruning when it can be lightly pricked into the surface with a fork, which also acts as a tidying up operation. The second application may conveniently be given when the first crop is over and the dead flowers removed. Excess dressings, particularly of nitrogenous fertilizers, are best avoided, otherwise soft sappy growths are produced late in the season, and these are generally more susceptible to fungal diseases.

Most growers consider mulching worth while, helping to retain moisture and smothering weeds. If farmyard manure is used it will make a nutrient contribution as well. Peat is now popular, compost can be used, as can lawn mowings if not applied too thickly. Lawn mowings should be used with caution, because you may also get a secondary crop of grasses and weeds, and there may also be other undesirable effects if the lawn has been treated with a selective weedkiller. Bark fibre, like peat, has little if any nutritional value but has become popular, possibly because of its nice appearance. Applied as a mulch it does not need any additional fertilizer.

Chemical means of weed control are also available, such as paraquat, used when there are no other plants growing between the bushes. Great care is required to ensure the liquid does not come in contact with the roses. Paraquat is more effective as a contact herbicide if used in conjunction with simazine.

Simazine is used effectively by many rose growers by applying in spring on clean ground which is still moist. It is residual in effect and keeps the soil clear of annual weeds, if the surface is not disturbed. Simazine does not harm the rose bushes.

Weed control is important, even if only to keep the garden tidy. Weeds compete for moisture and food and can act as hosts to some pests and diseases, so justifying the use of chemicals for their control.

Newly planted roses will require a good soaking of water if their first growing season is dry. In many gardens nowadays water is laid on either for the garden or garage, and mechanical methods of watering are available at lower cost than labour.

At the RHS Garden at Wisley a "cocktail" spray is applied every 10 to 14 days in the summer, containing a pesticide (dimethoate) and a fungicide (triforine) for controlling aphids, black spot and mildew, together with a foliar feed. (For further details on pests and diseases see pp.44-47).

Summer pruning or dead heading is a pleasurable chore for summer evenings. The removal of the old flower stems at the top leaf will ensure quick replacement with most modern cultivars. Disbudding is not essential unless special blooms are required, then the main bud is generally retained and the side buds removed when they are large enough to rub out.

Cutting roses for decoration is a form of summer pruning, the length of stem is of some importance as it is imperative to leave one or two eyes at the base to allow replacement growths for the provision of more blooms later. For large bowls or vases long stems are essential and suitable varieties will be required (see p.42). A counsel of perfection would be to cut only the length of stem required; the harder you cut, the longer the time required for replacement.

The bush rose, bought from a nurseryman, is a two part plant, i.e. the part which produces the flowers is growing on the roots of another plant. There are exceptions, some miniature roses sold are grown on their own roots, having being raised from cuttings. The root is known as the stock or sometimes root-stock; this is usually grown from seed, so producing better rooted plants which are less likely to contain virus. The advantages of this system are a better and more even crop of trees for supply to the rose-loving public and much more rapid multiplication of plants. From one plant a grower can get some fifty eyes or buds, each a potential plant, whereas from cuttings possibly one third of that number is produced. There is also greater certainty of a crop by budding, because many cultivars root poorly from cuttings, only ramblers and miniatures in general are reasonably successful.

The great advantage of roses grown on their own roots, i.e. vegetatively produced from cuttings, is that no "suckers" are produced, any growths produced being the parent plant. Budded roses may, however, produce growths below the point of union, i.e. from the roots; these are known as suckers. They should always be removed, as soon as they are seen, as they grow away from the roots and are thus nearer to the supply of plant food. Left alone weakening of the named plant occurs and sometimes it may eventually be completely overwhelmed. Any growth which occurs below the union of the stock and named plant is a sucker and should be pulled away, not cut. In particular, if *rugosa* stocks are planted too deeply there will be more trouble with suckers. These suckers generally have lighter coloured leaves which are also narrow and more numerous. Standards, which are usually budded on *R. rugosa* stocks, are inclined to produce suckers, and the leaves of these are dull green and quite different in appearance from the rose itself. If in doubt trace back the growth to its source, removing enough soil to do so; if it is growing from below the union bulge, it is a sucker. Some care is necessary when removing suckers from recently planted, but not properly established roses. Before pulling or wrenching the sucker away, keep the plant firmly in its place with your foot; this will prevent root damage.

Special tools are available for sucker removal, but these should be carefully used to avoid pruning (i.e. cutting) which results in the production of more suckers, probably in the ratio of three to one.

# 7. Propagation

Roses can be propagated from cuttings, and as such plants are on their own roots there is no danger of suckers being produced. If growths do arise from under the soil they will all be of the parent plant. Commercially, growing from hardwood cuttings rooted outdoors is not a viable proposition because of the amount of material required and even more because good saleable plants cannot be produced in a short time.

Varieties which grow readily from cuttings are ramblers such as 'American Pillar', cluster flowered bush roses which produce firm well ripened wood and some large flowered bush roses. Some varieties of the latter are inclined to produce pithy growths that do not root satisfactorily. Autumn is the best time (late September and early October) to take the cuttings using well ripened pencil-thick growths 9 inches (22cm) long. Cut them off with a sharp knife just under a node or leaf joint. Treat the cuttings with a rooting powder suitable for hardwood cuttings and remove all leaves except three at the top. In a border in a sheltered site, take out a small trench, cover the bottom with a layer of sharp sand and place the cuttings on the sand 6 inches (15cm) apart. Fill in the trench making the soil firm. If a number of plants are required, allow 1 foot (30cm) between the rows and leave the plants there until the following autumn, when they should be well rooted.

# 8. Plants in association with roses

More and more gardeners now prefer to grow other plants with their roses, for a whole garden of roses however glorious in high summer is a dull and dismal prospect during the months of winter. I prefer to look out of a window in February and to see the snowdrop, *Galanthus nivalis* or its more spectacular variety 'Atkinsii' growing near the edge of the bed in preference to bare soil. Other early spring flowers such as small-flowered crocuses or the dwarf narcissi, few are more delightful than 'February Gold' or 'Tête-a-Tête'. An odd plant of *Cyclamen hederifolium*, especially the white form, is a joy even when not in flower, the marbled leaves provide a most decorative carpet of ground cover. Auriculas also thrive with roses and many other plants, indeed some will overdo it and have a smothering effect, care must be taken to avoid planting rampant ground coverers.

I like roses grown in mixed borders, you can then plant some of the hardy geraniums such as 'Johnson's Blue' to provide wrappings for some of the shrub roses or such upright growers as 'Alexander' and 'Queen Elizabeth'. The lady's mantle, *Alchemilla mollis*, is a charming stand-by often choosing its own spot to grow with self sown seedlings. Violas in the past made a favourite accompaniment for roses, but alas are difficult to grow in hot summers in southern gardens although worth trying in cooler areas.

Silver leaved plants are always useful, especially as a foil to the more strident colours, for example the flowerless form of *Stachys* called 'Silver Carpet', is especially good in summer, though apt to look a bit tatty in winter. The late flowering *Crocus speciosus* is a delight in September and certainly unlikely to harm the roses.

# 9. A selection of roses

### Large flowered bush roses (Hybrid Teas)
The World Federation of Rose Societies has decided that as the original tea rose "blood" is no longer present in today's roses, it is no longer appropriate to retain the name Hybrid Tea for large-flowered roses. The large flowered rose is the aristocrat, producing high quality flowers of good form, large and high centred, and still most popular with the public in general. Most cultivars are free flowering enough to provide a good display in the garden, either moderately disbudded or allowed to flower naturally. Some given high cultivation and severely disbudded produce blooms ideal for exhibition while most are good for cutting for home decoration.

The name and date after the rose name in the list below refers to the raiser, usually the introducer, and the year in which the rose was introduced.

**Alec's Red** (Cocker 1970). 3ft (0.9m). Vigorous and upright in growth. The large full blooms are cherry red in colour, gloriously scented and freely produced, sometimes in large trusses, particularly in autumn.

**Alpine Sunset** (Cant 1975). 2½ft (0.8m). A sturdy medium grower. Large full flowers of creamy yellow flushed peach pink are freely produced in distinct crops and are fragrant.

**Alexander** (Harkness 1972). Up to 5ft (1.5m). A tall bold grower, suitable for large beds or hedges or for cutting with long stems. The flowers are somewhat thin but a glorious vermilion orange, luminous in their brilliance of display, slightly fragrant.

**Blessings** (Gregory 1967). 3ft (0.9m). A fine bedding variety, producing its shapely, soft coral pink flowers, with great freedom over a long season. Good for cutting also and possessing some fragrance.

**Diorama** (de Ruiter 1965). 3ft (0.9m). A variety which resists rain and is good for garden display especially in autumn. Rich apricot yellow, the flowers are fragrant, shapely and nice for cutting.

**Double Delight** (Swim and Ellis 1977). An eye catcher because of its colour, creamy white edged strawberry red. Fragrant.

**Elizabeth Harkness** (Harkness 1969). 2½ft (0.8m). A bushy grower, producing its creamy buff flowers early, perfectly formed with a tendency to apricot in autumn. Sweetly scented. A variety which does well in good weather.

**Fragrant Cloud** (Tantau 1964). 3ft (0.9m). A variety very highly rated for some years for its glorious scent. Many admirers have now become more critical as its geranium red flowers change to purplish red, especially in hot weather. Autumn brings some improvement but a tendency to black spot as well.

**Grandpa Dickson** (Dickson 1966). 3ft (0.9m). An upright grower, requiring fairly close planting for garden effect. The cool lemon yellow blooms have red flushes in autumn, are of classical shape and good size. Exceptionally beautiful if grown under glass and also an exhibitor's favourite.

**Just Joey** (Cant 1973). 2½ft (0.8m). A good bedding rose of spreading habit and very free flowering. A popular rose because of its unique coppery orange colouring with light and deep flushes difficult to describe but always lovely.

**Lovers Meeting** (Gandy 1980). Tall growing with flowers of a new shade of orange. The bronzy foliage compliments the distinctive colour.

**Mischief** (McGredy 1961). 3ft (0.9m). One of our best roses for garden display, resistant to bad weather and very free flowering. The soft coral salmon blooms deepen in autumn and are in general of medium size and good form. Occasionally a super bloom is produced, suitable for exhibition.

**Mullard Jubilee** (McGredy 1969). Up to 4ft (1.2m). A superb bedding rose which should not be planted less than 2½ft (0.8m) apart, being very vigorous in growth. The large deep rose pink flowers are shapely and fragrant.

**National Trust** (McGredy 1969). 2½ft (0.8m). A most compact bushy grower, of ideal habit and with nice coppery red foliage when young. The deep crimson red blooms are produced with the utmost freedom and are shapely but unfortunately have little scent. Nevertheless a fine garden rose for effective display.

**Pascali** (Lens 1963). 3½ft (1.1m). Tall and upright in growth, the medium sized flowers are white shaded cream in the centre and generally produced singly on long stems. Being of good form and substance it is one of the best for cutting and as a bedder stands up to wet weather reasonably well.

**Piccadilly** (McGredy 1960). 3ft (0.9m). A very popular bicolour of scintillating beauty, scarlet with pale yellow reverse. First class for bedding being very free flowering over a lengthy season, and weather resistant. Has given several sports, the most distinctive being named after the late Harry Wheatcroft, a flamboyant character in the rose world. The flowers are orange striped yellow, but somewhat variable according to the season.

**Pink Favourite** (Abrams 1956). 3ft (0.9m). A vigorous rose, excellent for bedding and noted especially for its handsome foliage which is most disease resistant. The large flowers are shapely, clear rose-pink which deepens on outside petals and fades slightly with age. When disbudded and given good cultivation it provides handsome exhibition blooms.

**Pot o'Gold** (Dickson 1980) 3ft (0.9m). Vigorous and bushy, freely producing its flowers of old gold. Aptly named and sweetly fragrant.

**Precious Platinum** (Dickson 1974). 4ft (1.2m). A very vigorous bedding rose which flowers with great freedom but should not be planted closely; 2½ft (80cm) seems ideal. The well formed blooms are brilliant deep red and seem reasonably weather resistant.

**Red Devil** (Dickson 1967). 4ft (1.2m). A rose of the utmost vigour, handsome in its foliage, tinted crimson when young. The fragrant, crimson scarlet blooms have a lighter reverse, are very full and high centred, the answer to the exhibitor's prayers. But it is intolerant of heavy rain so should not be planted for garden decoration in areas of high rainfall. Plant 2½ft (80cm) apart.

**Rose Gaujard** (Gaujard 1957). 4ft (1.2m). A tough healthy rose, ideal for the beginner being easier to grow than some in this section, making a large plant and being a prolific producer of flowers. These are large, carmine rose with silvery white reverse. Although somewhat garish in colour and producing many split blooms, its advantage is that it is a very healthy rose.

**Rosy Cheeks** (Anderson 1975). Compact grower, freely producing showy flowers, red with a yellow reverse. A fragrant bicolour.

**Silver Jubilee** (Cocker 1978). 2½ft (0.8m). A handsome newcomer of good upright habit, producing its flowers with great freedom over a long season, usually borne singly on short stems. Complex in colour but described officially as coppery salmon pink with peach shadings. With a slight fragrance, this variety seems destined to create fresh interest for its beauty not only in the garden but especially when grown under glass. May require protection against black spot in bad areas.

**Sunblest** (Tantau 1973). 3ft (0.9m). A vigorous, upright grower which produces medium sized flowers of unfading golden yellow in abundance. Slightly fragrant with long straight stems which are useful for cutting.

**Troika** (Poulsen 1972). 3ft (0.9m). A fine vigorous variety, very well suited to garden decoration or for cutting. Shapely flowers of an attractive apricot to orange bronze are freely produced and fragrant.

**Wendy Cussons** (Gregory 1959). 4ft (up to 1.2m). A strong reliable grower with a wonderful habit which not only makes a fine bedder but is good for standards. The large shapely flowers are sometimes described as carmine or cerise scarlet. It is not everyone's taste but popular generally because of its fine fragrance and reliability as a garden rose.

**Whisky Mac** (Tantau 1967). 3ft (0.9m). A rose which requires a good soil to produce a good plant being a somewhat poor grower when conditions do not suit it. In spite of this and a tendency to mildew it has acquired popularity through the glory of its apricot gold flowers of good form and considerable fragrance, which are delightful when cut.


## Cluster flowered bush roses (Floribunda)

This group of roses is much favoured for mass planting to provide colour over a long season especially in public gardens, but they are equally effective in private gardens where their continuity of flowering is only excelled by their mass production of bloom. The habit of flowering in trusses is diversified by blooms which may be single, semi-double or even of classical shape but with smaller individual blooms. Many varieties have a pleasing fragrance although in general this is not so easily discerned as in the large flowered roses. The cluster flowered roses have a distinct advantage in bad weather, because unopened buds remain undamaged and open in succession, thus keeping up the display. An important point for the beginner is their ease of cultivation and general hardiness.

**Allgold** (Le Grice 1956). 2½ft (0.8m). A compact grower with healthy foliage resistant to disease. The bright buttercup yellow flowers are remarkable for their stability of colour and resistance to rain. Flowers early and repeats quickly, but now requires good cultivation to keep up to standard.

**Arthur Bell** (McGredy 1965). 3ft (0.9m). A healthy grower which produces large bright yellow flowers freely. These fade to cream; they are weather resistant and fragrant, unusually so for this type of rose.

**Bonfire Night** (McGredy 1971). 3ft (0.9m). A good rose for bedding display where brilliant colour is required. The neatly formed flowers are bright orange with splashes of yellow and scarlet. Useful also as a cut flower.

**Dame of Sark** (Harkness 1976). 3ft (0.9m). A vigorous grower which produces rich orange flowers freely on a handsome plant. Very impressive for bedding.

**Elizabeth of Glamis** (McGredy 1964). 3ft (0.9m). A temperamental beauty, only suitable for warm sheltered gardens with good soil. In such a situation a joy to behold, its salmon pink flowers suffused apricot are fragrant also. May require protection against disease.

**Escapade** (Harkness 1967). 3ft (0.9m). A bushy grower ideal for display where its somewhat unusual colour is required. The large flowers are rosy magenta or violet and open out showing a white centre. Nearly always in bloom with a pleasing perfume, it is good for cutting, especially if done before the flowers have expanded.

**Evelyn Fison** (McGredy 1962). 2½ft (0.8m). One of our brightest bedding roses which has become popular because of its double vivid red flowers which are freely produced over a long season.

**Eye Paint** (McGredy 1976). 4ft (1.2m). A vigorous plant, which lightly pruned will assume the stature of a shrub. Single flowers of a beautiful scarlet with a yellowish white eye enhanced by the golden yellow stamens presents an unconventional but delightful appearance. May require protection against black spot in some areas.

**Glenfiddich** (Cocker 1976). 3ft (0.9m). Included because of its superb display in northern, cooler gardens. There its golden-amber shapely flowers are more beautiful than when grown in hotter, drier conditions. Upright in growth and lovely as a cut flower.

**Iceberg** (Kordes 1958). 4ft (1.2m). A famous rose, unsurpassed as a standard and pruned lightly will grow into a fine shrub. Pruned normally makes a fine bed, outstanding because of its freedom in production of its pure white flowers, which on occasion have a flush of pink. Very popular and useful as a background to other roses, useful also for hedges and for cutting. In some gardens protection against disease is necessary.

**Korresia** (Kordes 1973). 2½ft (0.8m). A bushy healthy grower which produces perfectly shaped golden yellow flowers which are fragrant. Regarded as the leading yellow rose in this section. Flowers are stable in colour and freely produced over a long season.

**Lilli Marleen** (Kordes 1959). 2½ft (0.8m). Compact in habit, this is a variety ideal for bedding. The scarlet red flowers are borne in profusion over a long season and are effective whatever the weather.

**Living Fire** (Gregory 1973). 3ft (0.9m). A vigorous upright healthy grower making an effective colourful bed. The orange flame flowers have a golden yellow base providing a luminosity that renders the name appropriate.

**Margaret Merril** (Harkness 1977). 3ft (0.9m). Medium in growth producing medium-size blooms of the most delicate blush sheen over white, not likely to appeal to those who desire a flamboyant garden display. Fragrant in addition to a nice form it is worth trying as a cut flower.

**Matangi** (McGredy1974). 2½ft (0.8m). A medium-sized, bushy grower which produces double orange vermilion blooms with a silver eye and reverse, profusely over a long period. One of a series called by the raiser "hand painted".

**Memento** (Dickson 1978). 2½ft (0.8m). A very neat rose with a compact habit of growth which makes it ideal for beds. The salmon-vermilion blooms open out flat, are very resistant to rain and freely produced.

**Moon Maiden** (Mattock 1970). 2ft (0.6m). Open and spreading in growth, the creamy yellow flowers are admirable for association with other roses in particular those of purple, mauve or lilac hue. Flowers particularly well in the autumn; a fine bedding rose.

**News** (Le Grice 1969). 2½ft (0.8m). Compact and robust in growth given good cultivation. The freely produced purple flowers deepen with age and associate well with 'Moon Maiden' (above).

**Picasso** (McGredy 1971). 2½ft (0.8m). The first of the "hand-painted" roses. Distinctive in its pattern of cherry red and white flower colour which fluctuates according to the season. The flowers are freely produced on slender growths, over an extended season even into November.

**Pink Parfait** (Swim 1960). 2½ft (0.8m). A most beautiful rose in form, in colour and surpassed by few as a prolific cropper. A creamy pink variable at some seasons but full of charm at all times and resistant to weather.

**Priscilla Burton** (McGredy 1978). 2½ft (0.8m). Another 'Picasso'-style rose with larger and better quality flowers. A vigorous grower with good foliage the blooms are deep carmine with a silver eye, lovely when fully expanded and in the bud stage. May require protection against black spot in some gardens.

**Queen Elizabeth** (Lammarts 1954). 5ft (1.5m) or more. A giant amongst bedding roses, full of vigour and easy to grow, not only in the British Isles, but in other countries too. The flowers are clear pink, profusely produced over a long season and weather resistant. The long stems are almost thornless so it is good for cutting. Ideal for a hedge if pruned to induce young basal growths to provide blooms on the sides rather than all on top. Must be carefully placed in small gardens as it outgrows most other varieties. Plant 3ft (90cm) apart.

**Rob Roy** (Cocker 1971). 3ft (0.9m). Upright in growth, a rose of superb crimson scarlet, freely produced; a spectacular bedder. A shapely flower and excellent under glass.

**Southampton** (Harkness 1972). 3ft (0.9m). One of the healthiest roses I know, unusually so for a rose of this colour. The apricot orange flowers are freely produced and have a pleasing scent. It is most useful for a large bed.

**Sue Lawley** (McGredy 1980). Vigorous grower. Attractive, slightly frilled flowers, edged light pink and white, deeper rosy pink towards centre, with a white eye.

**Sunsilk** (Fryer 1974). 2½ft (0.8m). A vigorous upright grower which produces a good crop of slightly fragrant lemon yellow blooms. A good variety for beds, flowering freely in late autumn. In bad areas may require protection against black spot.

**The Fairy** (Bentall 1932). 3ft (0.9m) but variable. A very healthy plant which starts to flower late but does so in profusion and over a long period. The small double flowers are a fresh soft pink in a delightful rosette formation and impervious to weather.

**Yesterday** (Harkness 1974). 3ft (0.9m). A plant which produces graceful growths combined with occasional long shoots, all producing small, fragrant flowers pink to lavender. Useful for a mixed border as well as the rose garden, blending in well with other plants.


I have kept a section of compact cluster flowered roses separate for the benefit of those with small gardens. Plant at 18 inches (45cm) apart.

**Anna Ford** (Harkness 1980). Low spreading grower, delightful orange red flowers and dainty leaves.

**City of Belfast** (McGredy 1968). 2½ft (0.8m). A fine low bedding rose producing bright vermilion scarlet flowers in nice trusses very freely.

**Esther Ofarim** (Kordes 1970). 1½ft (0.5m). A rose which requires good cultivation to grow really well. Very attractive brilliant flowers of orange vermilion with a gold base. Can be grown well under glass.

**Kim** (Harkness 1972). 1½ft (0.5m). Dwarf and very compact in growth, almost a cushion covered with canary yellow flowers sometimes flushed red.

**Marlena** (Kordes 1964). 1½ft (0.5m). Low and compact in growth, a ground cover plant with crimson scarlet flowers, often produced well into autumn.

**Meteor** (Kordes 1959). 1½ft (0.5m). A fine short grower with bright vermilion flowers. A most useful rose.

**Mrs Walter Burns** (Harkness 1977). A newcomer with an old world look which should appeal to lovers of the old roses. A healthy grower, producing warm rose pink flowers full of petals on a neat plant.

**Pineapple Poll** (Cocker 1970). 2ft (0.6m). A very showy variety, light orange with red shades and a spicy refreshing scent.

**Regensberg** (McGredy 1979). 1½ft (45cm). Low growing Picasso type rose, the double pink and white flowers are freely produced.

**Stargazer** (Harkness 1976). 1½ft (0.5m). A unique rose with brilliant orange scarlet single flowers with a golden zone, freely produced. I find this a little charmer.

**Tip Top** (Tantau 1963). 1½ft (0.5m). A very short grower with comparatively large flowers in a beautiful shade of salmon pink.

**Topsi** (Tantau 1972). 1½ft (0.5m). Low growing bushy plant producing brilliant orange scarlet flowers. Does better in good conditions, apt to suffer from die-back in severe winters. May require protection from black spot.

**Warrior** (Le Grice 1977). 1½ft (0.5m). A promising dwarf variety with double flowers of scarlet red.


## Miniature roses

These have increased greatly in popularity in recent years and are really replicas in most respects of bush roses, scaled down and with smaller leaves and thorns to match. They can be grown as other roses, although in my view appear overwhelmed if placed too near them.

Planted in a small garden by themselves or in a raised formal bed, bringing them nearer to eye level seems to be an ideal solution: or they can be grown in pots, window boxes or other containers provided adequate room is available for roots. I personally would not plant them in a rock garden as they look out of place.

Miniature roses are propagated by cuttings or by grafting on a suitable understock, providing plants of differing character in either case. Plants from cuttings are in general small and useful for pot culture, indeed are often sold in or from pots. Grafted plants are much stronger growing into larger plants but still attractive and are sold as bare root plants. Cultivation is as recommended for other roses and the same pests and diseases have to be guarded against. A food compost is required for plants in pots or containers and good drainage is essential. A large number of varieties are now available from specialist growers and new miniatures arrive annually of which the following are a short selection.

**Angela Rippon** (de Ruiter 1978). Dainty double flowers salmon pink.

**Baby Masquerade** (Tantau 1956). Yellow flowers flushed pink, continuously in flower.

**Darling Flame** (Meilland 1971). Rich vermilion.

**Easter Morning** (Moore 1960). Ivory white.

**Fashion Flame** (Moore 1977). Coral orange, an outstanding variety.

**Hula Girl** (Williams 1975). Blends of orange. Repeats well.

**Lavender Jewel** (Moore 1978). Soft lavender blooms and shapely buds.

**Magic Carrousel** (Moore 1972). White edged red, very distinctive.

**New Penny** (Moore 1962). Nice bush grower, salmon orange.

**Para Ti** (Pour Toi) (Meilland 1946). Dainty habit. White with hint of cream.

**Rosina** (Dot 1951). Classic shaped, bright yellow flowers freely borne.

**Stacey Sue** (Moore 1976). Perfect miniature blooms, soft pink.

**Starina** (Meilland 1965). Orange-scarlet and gold bicolour, very fine.

**Shrub roses: for flowers and hips**

Many shrub roses extend their beauty to late summer and autumn, providing a second season of beauty by gorgeous displays of fruits. The selection which follows will I hope induce planting of a shrub or two from a list which must be limited because of space.

**R. caudata.** A species from China growing to 10ft (3m), with single red flowers followed by hips, which are bright red and hang in bunches. Flask shaped, very fine but seldom seen in gardens.

**R. davidii.** A species from western China, up to 10ft (3m) in height. The single pink flowers are succeeded by hips in bunches, long and bright red and with long sepals.

**R. ×highdownensis.** May be a seedling from *R. moyesii*, certainly closely related, a large shrub up to 12ft (3.7m). Single light crimson flowers followed by magnificent hips, flask shaped, orange red and as good as any in this group.

**R. holodonta.** Closely allied to *R. moyesii*, regarded by some as a pink form under the name *rosea*. The single deep rose flowers give way for an abundant crop of bristly orange red hips, equally as fascinating as others in this group.

**R. moyesii 'Geranium',** a form selected from plants raised from seed at Wisley in 1938. The best plant for average sized gardens and is more compact in habit than its parent. The single flowers are a brighter scarlet red and even more spectacular hips.

**R. rubrifolia.** A fairly vigorous shrub up to 7ft (2m). Not renowned for its flowers which are rather small single cerise pink having little garden effect. However the red hips occur in great globular clusters, on arching branches. A great favourite with floral arrangers for its foliage, greyish green tinged purple and very effective in the garden.

**R. rugosa alba.** The large single white flowers are rendered more beautiful by the pale brown stamens quickly followed by the large tomato red hips. A handsome rounded shrub 5ft (1.5m) either way and like the others of this species easy to grow, healthy and decorative over a long season. **Frau Dagmar Hartopp** is a seedling from *R. rugosa*, often found in catalogues under the name "Frau Dagmar Hastrup". Not only the best *rugosa* for small gardens, usually around 4ft (1.2m) but also most beautiful. The delicate shell pink flowers are slightly cupped, the handsome hips deep tomato red. Delightful for a dwarf hedge, clipped in winter to an even height. **Scabrosa.** A large *rugosa* shrub 6ft (1.8m) either way, well worth planting in a large garden as a specimen or for a hedge. The very large single flowers are a rich crimson purple with tinges of violet, and produced continuously over the season. A vigorous plant, the hips are large tomato red and the flowers scented. Disease free as are all the *rugosa* roses.

**Scharlachglut** also known as 'Scarlet Fire' is a very vigorous, thorny shrub, requiring lots of room for its 8ft (2.4m) long arching growths. The

*Fig. 19. Above. Hips of Rosa caudata.*

*Fig. 20. Below. Hips of Rosa rugosa scabrosa.*

large scarlet crimson single flowers are handsome as are the large pear-shaped hips, orange scarlet lasting well into winter.

**R. setipoda.** A Chinese rose usually around 8ft (2.4m) high but upright in growth. The pale pink single flowers are scarcely as handsome as the beautiful hips but there is an added bonus because the leaves have the scent of sweet briar, less freely distributed over the air than *R. eglanteria*, our native sweet briar.

**R. sweginzowii.** Another species from China and a vigorous shrub up to 10ft (3m) high and nearly as much through. The rose pink flowers are single with a white centre, less decorative than the hips. These are bristly, flask shaped ripening early and provide a great spectacle in the garden. Very prickly.

### Shrub roses: recurrent flowering

Recurrent flowering shrub roses, are very effective in mixed borders or shrub-borders. Their habit of repeat flowering is of exceptional value in autumn.

**Angelina.** An attractive newcomer, which given good conditions may attain 4 feet (1.2m) either way. A delightful plant of dainty appearance, quite suitable for moderate sized gardens. The light pink semi-double flowers have prominent stamens adding to their charm and are produced over a long season.

**Ballerina.** A splendid small shrub 4ft (1.2m) tall. It fits well into a mixed border, but equally handsome if grouped or as a bed. Large clusters of small single delicate pink flowers with a white eye are freely produced, frequently on basal growths. I have seen very decorative standards of this rose.

**Belinda** is seldom seen in gardens but can be seen at Harlow Car (in Yorkshire) and the RNRS garden at St Albans. A shrub of some vigour growing 5ft (1.5m) high it produces clusters of soft pink flowers over a long season. It should not be confused with a cut-flower rose of the same name.

**Buff Beauty.** A most distinctive shrub up to 6ft (1.8m) on good soil or when trained against a wall. The arching growths are somewhat pendent in habit with nodding flowers varying from pale apricot to buff yellow. Flowering recurrent but often at its best in autumn and very fragrant.

**Chinatown.** A shrub of 5ft (1.5m) or over in height, of vigorous growth, useful as a hedge or as a background plant. Can be effective grown in a large bed if the long growths are pegged down. The large double flowers are deep yellow sometimes edged pink and are fragrant.

**Cornelia.** A fine shrub 5ft (1.5m) and upwards, growing into a thick bush. The semi-double flowers come in large clusters, apricot pink and subtly fragrant. The best flowers are produced in autumn when clusters are larger and colour deepens.

**Fountain.** A medium sized shrub 4ft (1.2m) and upwards. Very free flowering, the nicely shaped flowers are borne in clusters and are blood red in colour.

**Frank Naylor.** A distinctive newcomer 4ft (1.2m) and upwards, very attractive as the small leaves open in the spring when they are maroon coloured. The single flowers of deep crimson maroon have attractive golden centres, particularly good when seen close-up. May require protection against black spot.

**Fred Loads.** A very tall upright shrub up to 7ft (2.1m) in height. The large semi double light vermilion orange flowers are borne in large well formed trusses, so are valued by exhibitors. Has become popular also because of its freedom of flowering, bright colour, considerable vigour, and as a background rose.

**Golden Wings.** A rose which can be tailored to a medium sized garden by pruning hard but lightly pruned will attain 6ft (1.8m) either way. A delight for those who are lovers of the single flowered roses. The light primrose yellow flowers have a mass of buff yellow stamens as an additional attraction and are produced over a long period. Further value is provided by hips in a good autumn and by the fragrance of the flowers.

**Joseph's Coat.** A versatile shrub which by training may be induced to attain a height of 10ft (3m) as a climber but is normally a shrub around 6ft (1.8m) in height. Pruned severely it can be kept to around 4ft (1.2m) when it will produce a flamboyant display, especially in autumn. The changing colours denoted by its name are not universally favoured, but those who appreciate bright yellow, flushed with orange, changing to cherry-red, will find this very effective and bright.

**Kathleen Ferrier.** A shrub of medium vigour up to 5ft (1.5m) whose large semi-double salmon pink flowers borne in loose clusters are sweetly scented.

**Magenta.** Preferably grown as a shrub because its somewhat sprawly habit is not really suited to formal beds. The beautiful fully double flowers vary from lilac pink to soft deep mauve, often quartered in the manner of some of the old roses. Delightfully perfumed, the flowers are so freely produced as to weigh the growths down. A delight for floral arrangers who are partial to the subtle colour.

**Marjorie Fair.** A Harkness rose, bred from 'Ballerina' but much stronger in colour, really a crimson counterpart. With a height and spread of 4ft (1.2m) this variety seems destined to cheer up gardens with its wealth of colourful bloom.

**Penelope.** An attractive and popular shrub with pale apricot pink flowers which in full sunshine fade to white. Very free flowering on a plant 5ft (1.5m) high and wide and lovely for an informal hedge. Late flowers if not dead headed produce attractive smoky pink hips in a good autumn. In small gardens it can be pruned as a bedding rose. A rose worth its place for the fragrance, strong and musky.

**Shrub roses: summer flowering**

These are invaluable in gardens which are large enough to contain them. Once planted they are likely to remain for a considerable time, so it is worth while preparing the soil well. Many are so vigorous that given a good start they will thrive in gardens where gravel or chalk inhibit the bush roses. Modern shrub roses will mix quite well with bush roses, especially if used as a background. Useful also in mixed borders, where if roses are the main interest they may be allowed to dominate using ground covering herbaceous plants and bulbs towards the front. Hardy fuchsias are also useful for filling in gaps as are agapanthus, many of which are hardy and in the main blue, so providing a good contrast with any roses still in bloom. Shrub roses are somewhat bare during winter months so a few evergreen shrubs or trees where there is room should be used in the background. Such large shrub roses as 'Nevada' and its sport 'Marguerite Hilling' are really worth isolating as specimens standing in grass, although the branches usually provide their own ground cover when well grown, coming down to the ground when heavily studded with flowers.

**Canary Bird.** Flowering early each spring, generally in May, producing masses of single canary yellow, scented flowers. Plant 5ft (1.5m) apart to appreciate the arching branches, with delicate ferny leaves still decorative when flowers are over.

**Constance Spry.** Very vigorous with a spread and height up to 8ft (2.4m) and most effective if provided with some support. The large cupped flowers are magnificent glowing pink with a distinctive fragrance and are freely borne each summer.

**Fritz Nobis.** A shrub of medium vigour, with a height and spread 5ft (1.5m). A lovely rose with semi-double pale salmon pink flowers, sweetly scented and borne in abundance. A small bonus of round red fruits (hips) adds interest in autumn.

**Frühlingsgold.** A vigorous shrub with the great attribute of growing well in all types of soils so should not be planted more closely than 6ft (1.8m). It usually exceeds that in the height and spread of its branches. This rose is a superlative sight in May and early June when festooned with the large semi-double creamy yellow flowers. Added to this is its fragrance, which carries some distance.

**Frühlingsmorgen.** Fairly vigorous and somewhat sparse in growth but worth a place for its glorious single rose-pink flowers, enhanced by yellow centres, and dark stamens. Can attain 6ft (1.8m) in good soil and is scented.

**Golden Chersonese.** A beautiful addition to shrub roses attaining a height of 6ft (1.8m) or more in a sheltered position. Upright and graceful in growth it combines the best qualities of its parents, inheriting the deep gold from *R. ecae* and the larger flowers from 'Canary Bird'. The single flowers are fragrant, and are produced early and freely. Plant 5ft (1.5m) apart so as to enjoy the habit of this fine plant.

**Marguerite Hilling.** A wonderful sight when in its full flush of bloom like its parent 'Nevada' from which it is a sport, but in this case the flowers are light pink with flushes of deeper pink.

**Nevada.** Magnificent as a specimen, unsurpassed by any rose except its sport for sheer profusion of bloom. A large rounded shrub with a height and spread of 6ft (1.8m) and more on good soil. The arching stems are festooned with large semi-double creamy white flowers along their full length, often obscuring leaves and stems and when isolated reaching the ground. In good summers a few flowers appear later but never presenting their midsummer spectacle.

**R. x pteragonis Cantabrigiensis.** A fine easily grown shrub 7ft (2.1m). Single creamy yellow flowers abundantly produced. Flowers early and fine as a specimen shrub, having an elegant habit.

## Old roses

The old shrub roses delight many by their charm, form of flower and perhaps most of all their scent. Many do not mix well with the stronger colours of modern roses, nor do they last so long in bloom, so are best planted in borders associated with other plants which will add interest when the roses are past their best. A small list will help beginners, collections can be seen in several gardens if a greater representation is required. Some continue to thrive in cottage gardens, indeed have done so for a long time and look very much at home there.

**Alba Maxima,** an antique but still vigorous and around 6ft (1.8m). The flat ivory white double flowers give a lavish display. Very hardy and will mix in any company. I have seen it used effectively on a north wall in a very exposed garden.

**Cardinal de Richelieu.** A gallica shrub well known for its dark velvety purple flowers on a plant up to 5ft (1.5m) in height. Fragrant and demanding good cultivation such as pruning after flowering and feeding generously.

**Cecile Brunner** is classed as a china rose and is a small shrub, suited to the smallest of gardens. A favourite with many for its tiny perfectly shaped miniature blooms of pale blush pink, deeper in the centre and scented. In larger gardens the sport 'Bloomfield Abundance', which will attain 6ft (1.8m), may be more satisfactory although not quite so refined. There is also 'Climbing Cecile Brunner' a recurrent and vigorous climber for walls in particular and remarkably free flowering.

**Celestial.** Sometimes called Celeste, lovely in bud and exquisite in bloom, clear rose pink perfectly complemented by the grey-green leaves. Grows to around 6ft (1.8m) therefore a large bush. A sweetly scented favourite.

**x centifolia muscosa.** The common moss with clear pink flowers, scented and with well mossed buds. Sentimentally has a considerable charm, especially in cottage gardens but offset by a tendency to mildew. Medium growth reaching about 4ft (1.2m).

**Complicata.** A beautiful single rose of unknown origin, one of my favourites. The large flowers are bright clear pink with a white centre and golden stamens. Grown as a shrub will reach 5ft (1.5m) each way but will attain more if given support, such as an old fruit tree. Very floriferous.

**Gallica officinalis.** The apothecary's rose and considered to be the red rose of Lancaster. Makes a shrub around 3½ft (1.1m), suckering freely and very much at home in cottage gardens. The semi-double flowers are bright crimson red with a purplish cast.

**Gallica versicolor.** 3½ft (1.1m) sport of the above recorded in the seventeenth century and often called "Rosa Mundi". Very striking in its semi-double flowers irregularly striped and splashed with blush white through the original red. Most floriferous and a great favourite. As a hedge it can be clipped hard, but is apt to get mildew in autumn.

**Mme Hardy.** A fairly vigorous damask rose up to 6ft (1.8m). Flowers in clusters become pure white with a small green eye. Regarded by many as the most beautiful of white roses.

**Petite de Hollande.** A centifolia with miniature flowers on a compact shrub 4ft (1.2m) tall. The double flowers of pale pink deepen towards the centre and are freely produced and scented. A charmer for small gardens.

**Tuscany.** A gallica shrub 4ft (1.2m), sometimes called the "Old Velvet Rose". Upright in growth, topped off with the deep purple crimson flowers in contrast to the large centre of golden stamens. A more double form with larger flowers 'Tuscany Superb' is probably a sport.

**Zephirine Drouhin.** The most famous bourbon rose and still remarkably popular, although mildew can be severe in autumn. Can be grown as a climber being vigorous, or pruned, as a large shrub or as a hedge. Vigorous and recurrent in bloom up to 10ft (3m), the cerise-carmine flowers are strongly scented. Almost free of thorns it has become popularly known as the "thornless rose".

**Climbers: summer flowering**
Summer flowering ramblers or climbers are useful for growing on fences, pergolas or walls where space is available. Being vigorous they must have plenty of room giving as a reward a generous display of bloom and in some varieties a few blooms later in the season.

**Alberic Barbier** is an old favourite; yellow buds becoming creamy white on opening, scented. Almost evergreen, it is a vigorous grower which does well in most aspects. 20ft (6.1m).

**Albertine** is still popular although prone to mildew when planted on walls. The copper pink buds open to fragrant salmon pink flowers which are generously displayed. A vigorous grower up to 15ft (4.6m).

**Crimson Shower** grows up to 8ft (2.4m) so is ideal for a pillar. The small double flowers are produced in clusters, in a deep glowing crimson. Ideal also for a weeping standard. Later flowering than most other roses.

**Elegance** is a vigorous climber around 15ft (4.6m). Magnificent when in full flush with its perfectly formed pale yellow scented flowers.

**Francois Juranville.** A beautiful climbing rose growing to about 15ft (4.6m). The double flowers open flat to a salmon coral pink, deeper towards the centre and fragrant. A good rose for a pergola with a few flowers later in the season.

**Lawrence Johnston** is a most spectacular early flowering rose, and can when happy attain a height of 20ft (6m). The semi-double bright yellow scented flowers are luxuriantly produced, with a second flush later.

**Mme Gregoire Staechelin.** Flowers early in June. The large, sumptuous pink blooms are scented and produce large hips if not dead headed. It is a vigorous rose, to 15ft (4.6m).

**Pompon de Paris, Climbing** a climbing miniature, which reaches at least 15ft (4.6m). Lovely when smothered with its miniature double rose pink flowers.

**Sanders White Rambler** is an effective rambler for pergola, pillar or as a weeping standard. The small double white flowers are beautiful, freely produced and scented.

## Climbing roses: recurrent flowering

Climbing roses, which are recurrent flowering and have largely replaced the older climbers because of a longer flowering season. Useful for covering fences, pillars and walls.

**Altissimo,** a large single blood red crimson flowered rose 6ft (1.8m) or a little more. Very distinct.

**Bantry Bay,** a vigorous climber which flowers profusely. The semi-double light rose pink flowers are produced on a plant 10ft (3m) high.

**Compassion.** A fairly vigorous climber breaking freely from the base and reaching around 10ft (3m) high. Light salmon pink flowers with apricot shadings and deeply fragrant. 'Compassion' has produced a primrose yellow sport, 'Highfield'.

**Danse du Feu.** Fairly vigorous up to 10ft (3m) making a vivid splash of colour. Bright scarlet crimson flowers when at their best, turning purplish with age and freely produced.

**Golden Showers.** A climber which is nearly always in bloom, growing to around 6ft (1.8m) or higher on a wall. The bright yellow flowers are open and sweetly scented, useful as a pillar rose.

**Handel** is a fine climber up to 10ft (3m) which breaks freely from the base. The moderately full flowers are shapely in bud, opening cream flushed pink and red especially at edges, an attractive combination. Should be watched for black spot.

**Leverkusen,** a Kordesii hybrid up to 10ft (3m). Valuable for its healthy growth, freedom of flower production and its good pale yellow colour.

**Mermaid.** Surely the rose that is best for continuous flowering, which when happy can attain 25ft (7.6m) or more on a warm wall. The large single sulphur yellow flowers are much enhanced by the amber stamens. Does not like much pruning, so requires room to do it justice.

**Morning Jewel.** A free growing cultivar up to 8ft (2.4m) which produces rich glowing pink flowers freely. Breaks freely from the base. Fragrant.

**New Dawn,** a climber up to 12ft (3.7m) if trained, but quite happy as a shrub. The pale blush silvery pink flowers fade in hot weather to blush white and are sweetly fragrant. Useful also as a hedge.

**Parkdirektor Riggers.** A vigorous Kordesii climber which is most effective when covered with its unfading deep crimson flowers. It is apt to get mildew and blackspot when grown against a wall.

**Pink Perpetue.** A rose which has become popular because of its free flowering habit. It will attain a height of 6ft (1.8m) or a little more, so is ideal for pillars or fences. The medium sized flowers are bright rose pink, inclined to carmine on the outside.

**Ritter von Barmstede.** A vigorous Kordesii climber most suitable as a pillar rose. Grows to 10ft (3m). Semi-double flowers are deep cerise pink.

**Schoolgirl.** A beautiful climber of vigorous growth and has soft coppery-apricot fragrant blooms.

**White Cockade** is a climber (6-8 feet: 1.8-2.4m), with pleasantly scented lovely white flowers freely produced. Useful also as a shrub.

### Roses for cutting

Several of the roses recommended for garden decoration are useful and delightful as cut flowers. However some gardeners do not like cutting their garden display and prefer to devote some plants especially to the supply of flowers for house decoration. Suggestions are given below.

Roses are best cut at dusk or early morning and placed in a deep container so that most if not all the foliage can be covered for several hours. Proprietary materials are available which help to extend the life of the cut blooms. After a good soaking, blooms can be stripped of leaves and thorns and put back into the container until required.

**Anne Cocker.** A cluster flowered rose up to 4ft (1.2m) high. It is rather late flowering, but has proved valuable for cutting because of its long lasting qualities. Neat, shapely bright vermilion flowers. Should be watched for mildew.

**Corso.** A seedling from 'Anne Cocker' growing to 3ft (0.9m). Beautifully formed flowers of bright orange. Long lasting when cut and good for under glass.

**Dr A. J. Verhage.** A rose of medium vigour growing to 2ft (60cm), which requires a sheltered position outdoors. A delight when grown under glass, shapely flowers, rich yellow touched bronze and scented.

**Fairy Dancers.** A small flowered, short variety 2ft (60cm) which is ideal for small arrangements. The blush pink flowers in small sprays are shaded apricot in the most charming manner and are scented.

**Iced Ginger.** Cluster flowered and of upright growth 3ft (90cm). Lovely shapely buds, apricot buff with deep copper tints, beautiful and long lasting.

**King's Ransom.** Fairly vigorous; 3ft (90cm). The medium sized flowers are rich yellow, nicely formed with a slight scent and it flowers freely.

**Korp.** A vigorous upright grower; 3ft (90cm). Difficult to excel for brightness, neatly shaped, bright vermilion flowers, produced singly as a rule on good stems, lasting well when cut, and holding its colour well. Known also as 'Prominent'.

**Maud Cole** is a rose for those who like something unusual in colour, a deep mauve purple with striking dark foliage in harmony. Slightly scented and 2½ft (0.8m) high.

**Ophelia.** A famous rose about 3ft (0.9m) in height; the progenitor, mainly through sports, of many rose varieties which have been valued as cut flowers, in particular when grown under glass. 'Ophelia' is pale blush in colour with a hint of yellow; 'Mme Butterfly' one of its sports, is somewhat deeper, a pale pink. 'Lady Sylvia', clear pink, is a sport from 'Mme Butterfly', the deepest of the three. All are worth growing as cut flowers and have long been favourites having a refined appearance and a glorious fragrance. Apt to suffer damage to the blooms from thrips.

**Sea Pearl.** An upright cluster flowered rose 3½ft (1.1m) producing shapely flowers, somewhat variable but attractive in shades of salmon pink and peach and are long lasting with some fragrance.

**Sutter's Gold** is a particular favourite of mine; 3ft (0.9m), which is slow to establish. Lovely in its deep orange and red buds, which open to light yellow flushed pink flowers, pleasantly fragrant. Flowers not long lasting but prolifically produced, especially the first crop so replacement is easy. Early flowering and has nice, long stems.

**Sweet Promise** is a fine rose for cutting especially when grown under glass. It is generally sold in shops as 'Sonia'. Grown outside will attain 3ft (0.9m), but does not care for a wet summer. The lovely shapely flowers are salmon pink produced on clean smooth stems.

**Garnette** and its progeny have in the main rather stiff petals which have remarkable lasting power when cut. Can be grown outside, but are better for cutting when grown under glass.

## Roses for walls (see also pp.40-42)

Climbing roses have been used for many years for growing against house walls, judging by the evident age of many the specimens which can be seen. Walls facing south and west are very suitable for growing some of the slightly tender and choice roses.

**Alba Maxima.** The "Great Double White" or "Jacobite Rose" although shrubby in growth succeeds very well on a north wall and given some support to the main branches can attain 8ft (2.4m). From these, branches arch outwards which are festooned with the creamy white flowers, against a background of glaucous foliage.

43

**Alba Semi-plena,** generally supposed to the "White Rose of York" is even more vigorous, up to 10ft (3m) especially if trained to a wall. The semi-double flowers are freely borne and are succeeded in due course by a handsome display of hips.

**Alberic Barbier,** one of the best known climbers which puts up a good performance even in an unkind situation.

**Dortmund,** a Kordesii hybrid which attains 10ft (3m) and is recurrent flowering especially if dead headed to prevent a crop of hips. The single red flowers have a white eye which surrounds the boss of yellow stamens and are carried in large clusters.

**Felicite et Perpetue,** an extremely hardy climber, around 12ft (3.7m) which benefits from light pruning, cutting out old wood and shortening back some growths after flowering. At flowering time there is a complete coverage of small rosette milk white flowers with flecks of red which are pleasantly scented. Frequently to be seen in old gardens and remains a distinctive and beautiful rose.

**Golden Showers** which has already been commended (p.41) is also useful for growing on a north wall.

**Mme Alfred Carriere** a climber just a century in age but still full of vigour, reaching 20ft (6.1m). The double white flowers are flushed pink.

**Parade,** a vigorous climber of 12ft (3.7m) with large very double scented flowers which are borne very freely in clusters, inclined to droop which is an asset when above head height. Colour is variable, rose red to carmine.

**Veilchenblau,** a vigorous rose up to 15ft (4.6m), often referred to as the "blue" rose but more purple-violet maturing to lilac grey; an unusual colour which does not always generate approval. However beauty is in the eye of the beholder, so those who appreciate this rose will find it retains its colour better in a shaded aspect, than full sun.

# 10. Diseases

Most forms of life are subject to pests and diseases and roses have their quota, so it is fortunate for the rose grower that means exist for their control. Good cultivation, already advocated for other reasons, is also important, as healthy trees growing in good conditions are less liable to attack. It is important to watch for early signs of any infection, and apply remedial measures early.

Most gardeners find it necessary to take preventive action against diseases and some common sense precautions are necessary. To prevent germination of the disease spores it is necessary to keep both sides of the leaves covered with a coating of fungicide. When roses are in active growth this means fortnightly applications to ensure protection of new leaves, but timing can be altered according to weather conditions. For instance after heavy rain renewal of the protective cover becomes necessary. Some new fungicides are absorbed into the plant tissues to give internal protection against fungi.

Sprays in general give more effective protection than dusts, but should not be used in hot sunshine. The best time is a calm dry evening. Better coverage is obtained when chemicals are mixed with rainwater. All materials should be used according to the makers directions and all should be treated with respect, and a pair of rubber gloves to protect hands is an elementary but often neglected precaution.

**Black spot** appears on the lower leaves of the rose bush like a splash of ink with fringed edges. It can appear as early as May, but is most noticeable from early August on to October, especially if hot humid weather has been prevalent. Thus it is more common in the south western counties where weather conditions are more favourable than elsewhere. Those who live in industrial areas seldom if ever see this disease, but the extension of smokeless zones will I fear lead to greater familiarity with its appearance. Attacks vary in severity according to season and area and when severe, defoliation takes place in autumn with a weakening effect on the bushes. Protection before infection is all important and the bushes should, therefore, be sprayed immediately after spring pruning with a fungicide such as dichlofluanid, maneb, captan or zineb. Then spray the bushes at regular intervals throughout the summer. The partially systemic fungicides benomyl and thiophanate-methyl will also control black spot but regular use of these fungicides may lead to the development of tolerant strains of the fungus. However, no resistance has yet been found against triforine, a newer fungicide of this type. As the disease is worse on weak bushes, a foliar feed applied during the summer will improve their vigour and resistance. The disease overwinters on the leaves and these should be raked up and burnt.

**Powdery mildew** is an easily recognised disease, the young growths and leaves being covered with a dust which presents a flour-sprinkled appearance, in bad attacks becoming almost felt-like. This disease occurs all over the country, especially in dry seasons, and is often most noticeable in certain cultivars planted close to walls where little rain may fall. The disease can be prevented to a certain extent in these positions by mulching to conserve moisture and by watering in dry periods before the soil dries out completely. Some cultivars are more susceptible and in mildew-prone areas these should be avoided. The well-known rambler 'Dorothy Perkins' has become notorious. Fortunately resistant cultivars are available.

Powdery mildew can be controlled by spraying with dinocap or the partially systemic fungicides bupirimate with triforine, benomyl, carbendazim and thiophanate-methyl but the fungus could become resistant against the three latter fungicides which are related.

**Rose rust** flourishes in conditions similar to those which suit black spot but bad attacks are much more damaging to the plants. The orange coloured or rusty spores appear as pustules on the underside of the leaves. Later these turn black, the leaves lose their healthy appearance, becoming dry and brittle and fall off prematurely. In early and severe attacks trees may become weakened to such an extent as to warrant removal to prevent an extension of the attack. Discarded trees should be burnt as should all diseased leaves. Maneb, zineb and thiram have proved to give some control of rose rust but the most effective fungicide is oxycarboxin which is only available in commercial packs under the proprietary name of 'Plantvax'. However, the partially systemic fungicide triforine which is available only in combination with bupirimate, may also give a good control of rose rust.

**Canker,** which usually shows as rotting of the tissues at the base of a shoot, can be due to several different fungi but these generally attack only through wounds such as those caused by frost or poor pruning. However, plants lacking in vigour due to poor growing conditions may also be infected. Affected shoots die back as a result of the cankers and should be cut out. Dust the crowns of diseased plants with dry bordeaux powder.

**Dieback** of shoots can also be due to a number of other causes such as frost, too wet or too dry soil and malnutrition. It may occur in newly planted roses if the roots were not well spread out at planting or planting was too deep or shallow. It can be prevented, therefore, by making sure roses are planted correctly and are well fed and cared for. Failure of new roses also occurs when they are replanted in the same position as old ones because the soil has become "rose-sick". The only treatment for this trouble is to sterilize the soil with formaldehyde (for rate of application see below), or change it completely to a depth of about 2 feet (60cm) before replanting.

**Honey fungus** is a very common trouble on roses but unfortunately, this root parasite is not usually noticed until an affected plant dies suddenly. The fungus attacks from the soil and spreads as sheets of white fan-shaped growths beneath the bark on the larger roots and around the base of the stem. Brownish black root-like structures known as rhizomorphs develop on diseased roots and grow out through the soil and infect other plants. It is essential, therefore, to remove dead and dying plants together with as many roots as possible, before the fungus spreads too far. After removal, the soil should be sterilised with a 2% solution of formaldehyde i.e. 1 pint in 6 gallons of water (60ml in 30 litres) applied at the rate of 5 gal. to 1 sq. yd (27 litres per m²) or the soil should be changed completely before replanting. A proprietary product containing a phenolic emulsion could also be used.

**Leaf discoloration** can be caused by many factors such as cold wind, mineral deficiencies and spray injury. The damage is often temporary but if it persists specialist advice should be sought.

**Spray damage** due to the effects of misusing hormone weed-killers commonly occurs on roses and shows as distortion of the stem and leaf stalks which twist spirally and also of the leaves which become narrow and twisted or cupped and which show parallel veining. Such damage can be prevented by the careful use of hormone weedkillers which should only be applied with equipment kept specifically for their use. Affected plants usually recover in due course.

**Proliferation** affects only the flowers, particularly on old-fashioned bush roses. More flower-buds form within the centre of the bloom but generally remain small, green and hard. The cause is uncertain but in most cases is probably due to frost damage at a critical stage in the development of the flower bud. Cut off affected flowers. If the second crop is also affected and the trouble persists for several years it will probably be incurable.

# 11. Pests

Most prolific as well as most common of rose pests are **aphids,** better known as greenfly, although it has other guises, amber, reddish or black. Most people must be familiar with these small insects which cluster near the growing tips of young growths and around flower buds. Aphids breed rapidly so steps should be taken to eliminate them as soon as they are seen and they should not be allowed to become established. Using a fine spray of malathion or pirimicarb early in the season is effective especially if repeated after three days to catch any survivors. Excellent results which maintain control over a longer period have been obtained by the use of systemic insecticides such as formothion and dimethoate.

Possibly the most damaging pests of roses after greenfly are **caterpillars** which not only damage the leaves with their voracious feeding, but also attack buds as well. Many of these caterpillars become more active near dusk, a good time to walk round the garden. The time-honoured if somewhat messy technique of squeezing between finger and thumb is very effective in dealing with a few of these pests. Larger numbers should be sprayed with trichlorphon or dusted with carbaryl or fenitrothion.

The **leaf-rolling sawfly** gives a good deal of trouble in gardens surrounded by hedges, shrubs or trees where air is obstructed and the roses are shaded. Their presence is easily recognized as the leaves roll up laterally, spoiling their appearance as well as impairing their function and causing premature leaf fall. Spraying must be carried out to prevent the adult insects from laying their eggs, using trichlorphon or pirimphosmethyl. Three sprays between mid-May and mid-June should be effective.

The **rose slug sawfly** is also troublesome. The larva or "worm" is nearly transparent and devours the internal tissue of the leaf leaving a silvery skeleton, which looks unsightly. Spraying with trichlorphon or pirimphosmethyl is effective and may be required again in July or August when a second brood may hatch, especially if the earlier spraying was neglected.

**Leaf-cutter bees** cut neat semi-circular portions from the rose leaves. The damage done is seldom extensive enough to warrant any action against these relatively harmless insects.

**Thrips** or thunder flies are tiny insects which cause some damage during hot dry spells of weather. Mottling of leaves and distortion of young growths, plus discoloration along the edges of the rose petals are generally discernible to the eye of the keen rosarian. Pale pink roses particularly 'Ophelia' and its sports seem generally to be most susceptible. A systemic insecticide can be effective; malathion should also give some control.

Cuckoo-spit or common garden **frog-hopper** is easily recognized by the protective spittle-like mess surrounding the small yellow nymph which can easily be killed by finger and thumb when the numbers are few. They are frequently seen on other plants and on weeds also but can be disposed of by using a systemic or a contact spray such as malathion.

Some modern insecticides are cumulative in their effect and if intensive use is made of them pests may develop resistance. It is of some importance therefore to use insecticides in moderation. Roses generally can be kept reasonably clear of pests by a mid-May spray, followed by another a month later, and a final spray in early September.

**Rose leafhoppers** are small, pale yellow insects that live on the underside of the leaves. The nymphal stages are creamy white and less active than the adults, which tend to jump off the leaf when disturbed. Both adults and nymphs suck sap and this causes white or pale green spots on the upper surface of the leaves. Heavy attacks may occur on roses growing in warm situations, such as against a wall, and most of the leaves' green colour may be lost. Leafhoppers can be controlled by spraying thoroughly with a systemic insecticide when damage is first noticed.

**Red spider mite** is mainly a glasshouse problem but it can cause trouble on outdoor plants during hot dry summers or on roses growing in warm sheltered positions. The tiny, eight-legged mites are only just visible to the naked eye, and they occur on the underside of the leaves. Their colour is usually yellowish green rather than red. They suck sap from the foliage, which develops a fine mottled discoloration and later turns yellow and falls prematurely. Occasionally a fine silken webbing can be seen along the leaf margins and across the leaf axils. Red spider mite is difficult to control but three applications of a systemic insecticide at 7 to 10-day intervals when damage is seen should check the infestation.

*Printed in England*
*Cheney & Sons Ltd., Calthorpe St., Banbury*